Mrs Nidaa Alsubheen is an experienced Arabic teacher working in a primary school in the United Kingdom. Mrs Alsubheen holds a bachelor's degree in computer science. She lives in a friendly neighbourhood where her little kids enjoy playing and greeting people. Mrs Alsubheen is working on a series of short stories that aim to teach Arabic and English languages while emphasising moral ethics and the importance of family.

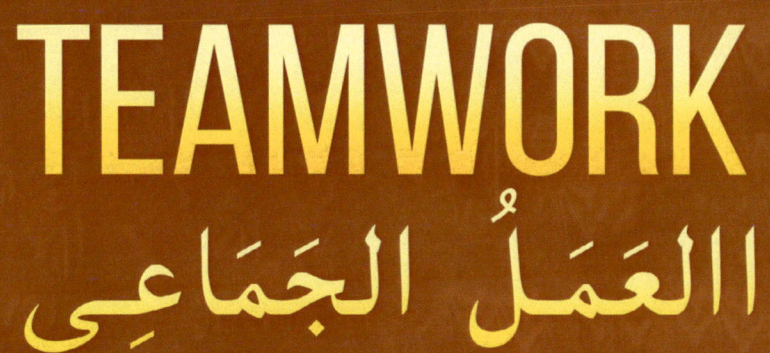

TEAMWORK
العَمَلُ الجَمَاعِي

WRITTEN BY
NIDAA
ALSUBHEEN

Austin Macauley Publishers™
LONDON · CAMBRIDGE · NEW YORK · SHARJAH

ILLUSTRATED BY
AMINA KENEWA

Copyright © Nidaa Alsubheen 2023
Illustrated by Amina Kenewa

The right of **Nidaa Alsubheen** and **Amina Kenewa** to be identified as author and illustrator of this work has been asserted by them in accordance with sections 77 and 78 of the Copyright, Designs and Patents Act 1988.

All rights reserved. No part of this publication may be reproduced, stored in a retrieval system, or transmitted in any form or by any means, electronic, mechanical, photocopying, recording, or otherwise, without the prior permission of the publishers.

Any person who commits any unauthorised act in relation to this publication may be liable to criminal prosecution and civil claims for damages.

A CIP catalogue record for this title is available from the British Library.

ISBN 9781398485631 (Paperback)
ISBN 9781398485648 (ePub e-book)

www.austinmacauley.com

First Published 2023
Austin Macauley Publishers Ltd®
1 Canada Square
Canary Wharf
London
E14 5AA

I would like to thank my sister Dr. Sana Alsubheen and her son Ahmad Ismail for reviewing the Arabic and English texts, Miss Bushra sharif and Miss Iman Elshennawy for editing the Arabic text, and Miss Maryam Kenewa for editing the English text of the story.

For teachers

To get the full extended benefit of this book, please follow these tips before reading:

- Discuss different predictions based on the front cover.
- Read the title in Arabic and in English.
- Flick through the book focusing on the illustrations. What do these illustrations depict?
- Use the (Words Index) to encourage reading of Arabic Words and English meanings.
- This story may take more than one session to read.
- Encourage learners to start reading Arabic paragraph first (more than once) and at their own pace, and then ask if they understand paragraph idea.
- If learners are struggling with the Arabic, ask them to read the paragraph in English, and then in Arabic again, (they can use the Words Index to help them to understand the Arabic terms).

بَيْنَمَا تَقُومُ لِينَا بِتَحْضِيرِ طَاوِلَةِ الطَّعَامِ لِأَرْبَعَةِ أَشْخَاصٍ تَمْتَمَتْ فِي نَفْسِهَا قَائِلَةً: هَذَا الْكُرْسِيُّ لِأُمِّي، وَهَذَا لِأَبِي، وَهَذَا لِيُوسُفَ، وَهَذَا لِي.. وَضَعَتْ لِكُلِّ وَاحِدٍ مِنْهُمْ صَحْنًا كَبِيرًا وَبِجَانِبِهِ مِلْعَقَةً وَشَوْكَةً وَسِكِّينًا.
أَحْضَرَتِ الْأُمُّ صِينِيَّةَ الطَّعَامِ، وَسَاعَدَهَا يُوسُفُ بِإِحْضَارِ قِنِّينَةِ الْمَاءِ وَالْأَكْوَابِ.

Whilst Leena was preparing the dining table for four people, she muttered to herself, "This chair is for Mother, this one is for Father, this one is for Yousef and this one is for me."
She carefully placed a large plate for each of them, adding a spoon, a fork and a knife beside it. Mother arranged the food tray and Yousef helped by bringing the bottle of water and cups.

جَلَسَ الجَمِيعُ فِي أَمَاكِنِهِم ثُمَّ سَأَلَ الأَبُ: مَا غَدَاؤُنَا اليَومَ؟

رَدَّتِ الأُمُّ: أَرُزٌّ مَعَ الدَّجَاجِ، وَبَعضُ البَاذِنجَانِ وَالكُوسَا وَالبَطَاطَا المَقلِيَّةِ.

قَالَ يُوسُفُ: أَنَا أُحِبُّ البَطَاطَا المَقلِيَّةَ.

احمَرَّ خَدَّا لِينَا ثُمَّ قَالَت: وَأَنَا حَضَّرتُ السَّلَطَةَ.

أَكَلَ الأَبُ مِنَ السَّلَطَةِ ثُمَّ قَالَ بِإِعجَابٍ: إِنَّهَا لَذِيذَةٌ! أَخبِرِينَا كَيفَ حَضَّرتِ السَّلَطَةَ؟

Everyone took their seat and Father excitedly asked, "What do we have for lunch today?"
"Rice with chicken and some fried aubergine, courgette, and potatoes,." Mother replied.
"I love fried potatoes!" Yousef exclaimed.
"I prepared the salad,." Leena mumbled shyly.
"It's delicious! Tell us how you prepared it,." Father declared admiringly after tasting the salad.

قَالَت لِينَا وَهِيَ تُحَرِّكُ يَدَيهَا: قَطَّعتُ الخِيَارَ وَالطَّمَاطِمَ وَالخَسَّ وَالفُلفُلَ الأَخضَرَ، ثُمَّ وَضَعتُ المِلحَ وَقَلِيلًا مِن عَصِيرِ اللَّيمُونِ.

ضَحِكَ الجَمِيعُ، وَقَالَ الأَبُ: أَحسَنتِ يَا لِينَا، ثُمَّ التَفَتَ إِلَى يُوسُفَ وَقَالَ: أُرِيدُ بَعضَ الخُبزِ مِن فَضلِكَ.

"I sliced some cucumber, tomato, lettuce and green pepper and dressed it with a pinch of salt and a drizzle of lemon juice,." she replied whilst shaking her hands excitedly. Everyone laughed.
"Well done, Leena!" Father exclaimed. "Yousef, could you pass me a piece of bread, please?"

انتَهَى الجَمِيعُ مِن تَناوُلِ الطَّعَامِ، وَقَالَ الأَبُ: كَانَ الطَّعَامُ لَذِيذًا، شُكرًا لَكُم.

رَدَّتِ الأُمُّ: عَلَى الرُّحبِ وَالسَّعَةِ.

حَمَلَ الأَبُ صَحنَهُ وَذَهَبَ بِهِ إِلَى المَطبَخِ، وَبَينَمَا الجَمِيعُ يُنَظِّفُونَ طَاوِلَةَ الطَّعَامِ دَقَّ جَرَسُ البَابِ، قَالَ يُوسُفُ: هَذَا صَدِيقِي أَحمَدُ.

Once everyone had finished eating, they began to clear up the table.
"The food was absolutely delicious, thank you!" Father said whilst taking his plate to the kitchen.
"You're welcome," Mother replied.
In that moment the doorbell rang. "It's my friend Ahmad!" Yousef yelled eagerly as soon as he opened the door.

قَالَ أَحْمَدُ: تَعَالَ نَلْعَبُ مَعًا يَا يُوسُفُ.

رَدَّ يُوسُفُ: مممممم.. أَعْتَذِرُ إِلَيْكَ يَا أَحْمَدُ، لَا أَسْتَطِيعُ اللَّعِبَ، اليَومَ سَأُسَاعِدُ أَبِي بِتَنْظِيفِ المَكْتَبَةِ.

سَأَلَ أَحْمَدُ مُسْتَغرِبًا: هَلْ تُسَاعِدُهُم فِي التَّنْظِيفِ؟!

"Come on, let's play outside," Ahmad suggested.
"Hmm, I'm sorry – I can't play today. I'm going to help Father clean the library," Yousef replied.
"You're helping with chores?" Ahmad asked with astonishment.

رَدَّ يُوسُفُ: نَعَم.. اليَومَ هُوَ يَومٌ نَتَعَاوَنُ فِيهِ عَلَى تَنظِيفِ البَيتِ وَإِعدَادِ الطَّعَامِ.

أَنزَلَ أَحمَدُ عَينَيهِ، وَقَالَ بِخَجَلٍ: أَنَا لَا أُسَاعِدُ وَالِدَيَّ.

سَمِعَ الأَبُ كَلَامَهُمَا، ثُمَّ قَالَ: تَعَالَوا يَا أَبنَائِي.. سَوفَ أَحكِي لَكُم قِصَّةً.

"Yes, today is the day we all work as a team to clean the house and prepare the food," Yousef replied.
Ahmad lowered his eyes shyly, "I don't help my parents."
Father heard their words and said, "Come on boys; I will tell you a story."

كَانَ يَا مَا كَانَ، فِي قَدِيمِ الزَّمَانِ، كَانَ هُنَاكَ بَعْضُ الأَصْدِقَاءِ يَعِيشُونَ مَعًا فِي مَزرَعَةٍ صَغِيرَةٍ تَقَعُ بِجَانِبِ نَهرٍ صَغِيرٍ، وَعَلَى الضِّفَّةِ الأُخْرَى غَابَةٌ جَمِيلَةٌ.

قَالَ الحِصَانُ الرَّمَادِيُّ: أُرِيدُ الذَّهَابَ إِلَى الغَابَةِ لِألعَبَ مَعَ النَّعَامَةِ وَالدُّبِّ ذِي الفَرْوِ البُنِّيِّ الجَمِيلِ.

"Long time ago in a faraway land, a group of animal friends lived together on a small farm next to a small river. On the other side of the river was a beautiful forest."
One day, the grey horse said, "I want to go to the forest to play with the ostrich and the beautiful brown, furry bear."

نَفَشَ الدِّيكُ الأَحْمَرُ رِيشَهُ، ثُمَّ قَالَ بِحَمَاسٍ وَهُوَ يَهُزُّ ذَيْلَهُ القَصِيرَ: وَأَنَا كَذَلِكَ.

حَرَّكَ الثَّوْرُ الأَسْوَدُ التُّرَابَ بِحَوَافِرِهِ، ثُمَّ سَأَلَ: وَأَنْتَ أَيُّهَا الحَمَلُ الأَبْيَضُ الصَّغِيرُ، هَلْ تُرَافِقُنَا؟

رَفَعَ الحَمَلُ قَرْنَيْهِ مُوَافِقًا.

سَأَلَتِ البَطَّةُ الصَّفْرَاءُ: هَلْ أَسْتَطِيعُ مُرَافَقَتَكُم؟

وَافَقَ الجَمِيعُ وَانْطَلَقُوا بِاتِّجَاهِ النَّهرِ..

"Me too!" the red rooster shouted excitedly whilst fluffing his feathers and wagging his short tail.
Pawing the ground with his hooves, the black bull looked up and asked, "What about you little lamb? Are you coming with us?"
The lamb nodded in acceptance.
"Could I please join you?" the yellow duck asked.
They all agreed and set off towards the river.

عَبَرَ الْأَصْدِقَاءُ النَّهْرَ، وَرَأَوُا النَّعَامَةَ ذَاتَ الرِّيشِ الْأَسْوَدِ وَالْبُنِّيِّ تَحْفُرُ بِمِنْقَارِهَا الْأَرْضَ تَبْحَثُ عَنْ بَعْضِ الطَّعَامِ.

صَاحَ الدِّيكُ: جِئْنَا نَلْعَبُ مَعَكِ أَيَّتُهَا النَّعَامَةُ.

فَرِحَتِ النَّعَامَةُ بِهِمْ، ثُمَّ قَالَتْ: لَكِنَّ الدُّبَّ مَشْغُولٌ الْيَوْمَ، وَلَا يَسْتَطِيعُ اللَّعِبَ مَعَنَا.

Once the animals crossed to the other side, they saw the black and brown-feathered Ostrich, digging the ground with its beak looking for something to eat.
"We came to play with you, Ostrich," the rooster crowed.
The Ostrich was happy to see them. "But Bear is busy today, he cannot play with us!" she said.

بَعدَ أَن لَعِبَ الجَمِيعُ مَعًا بِسَعَادَةٍ قَالَ الثَّورُ: لَقَد تَأَخَّرنَا، يَجِبُ أَن نَعُودَ إِلَى المَزرَعَةِ.

قَالَتِ النَّعَامَةُ: سَوفَ أُرَافِقُكُم إِلَى النَّهرِ.

So they all happily played together.
"We're late; we should go back to the farm," the bull suggested.
"I will accompany you to the river," the Ostrich said.

وَبَيْنَمَا هُم فِي الطَّرِيقِ كَانَتِ السُّلَحْفَاةُ البَطِيئَةُ تَمْشِي بِاتِّجَاهِهِم، ثُمَّ قَالَت وَهِيَ تَلْهَثُ: تَمَهَّلُوا يَا أَصْدِقَاءُ، لَا تَذْهَبُوا إِلَى النَّهرِ، هُنَاكَ تِمْسَاحٌ أَخْضَرُ مُفتَرِسٌ وَشِرِّيرٌ سَوفَ يُهَاجِمُكُم.

نَظَرَ الجَمِيعُ بِقَلَقٍ، ثُمَّ قَالَ الحَمَلُ: وَلَكِن هَذَا طَرِيقُ عَودَتِنَا الوَحِيدُ.

بَدَأَ الجَمِيعُ بِالتَّفكِيرِ لِحَلِّ هَذِهِ المُشكِلَةِ،

On their way, they saw the slow turtle walking towards them.
"Hold on, friends, do not go to the river!" she panted heavily. "There's an evil, savage, green crocodile that will attack you if you cross him," she added with a look of fear on her face.
They all looked on anxiously.
"But this is our only route to the farm," the lamb uttered.
Worriedly, they all began to think of a solution.

قَالَتِ البَطَّةُ: إِذَا تَعَاوَنَّا مَعًا سَوفَ نَعبُرُ النَّهرَ دُونَ أَن يُمسِكَ بِنَا التِّمسَاحُ، ثُمَّ أَضَافَت: أَنَا عِندِي جَنَاحَانِ، سَأَطِيرُ بِهِمَا وَأَحمِلُ بَعضَ الحِجَارَةِ بِمِنقَارِي وَأَرمِيهَا عَلَى التِّمسَاحِ لِإِلهَائِهِ.

"If we work as a team, we will cross the river without the crocodile catching us," the duck said emphatically. "I have two wings. I will fly and carry some stones with my beak and throw them at the crocodile to distract him."

هَزَّ الثَّوْرُ ذَيْلَهُ الطَّوِيلَ وَقَالَ: أَنَا عِنْدِي أَرْبَعُ أَرْجُلٍ قَوِيَّةٌ وَسَرِيعَةٌ.

وَقَالَ الحِصَانُ: وَأَنَا كَذَلِكَ سَرِيعٌ فِي الرَّكْضِ.

قَالَ الدِّيكُ بِحُزْنٍ: أَنَا عِنْدِي رِجْلَانِ صَغِيرَتَانِ، وَلَا أَسْتَطِيعُ الرَّكْضَ بِسُرْعَةٍ، وَعِنْدِي جَنَاحَانِ وَلَكِنْ لَا أَسْتَطِيعُ الطَّيَرَانَ.

وَقَالَ الحَمَلُ: أَنَا عِنْدِي أَرْبَعُ أَرْجُلٍ وَلَكِنِّي بَطِيءٌ.

قَالَ الحِصَانُ: سَوْفَ نَتَعَاوَنُ مَعًا، أَنَا سَأَحْمِلُ الدِّيكَ عَلَى ظَهْرِي، وَالثَّوْرُ سَيَحْمِلُ الحَمَلَ الصَّغِيرَ.

قَالَتِ النَّعَامَةُ: وَأَنَا سَأَبْحَثُ عَنِ الدُّبِّ لِيُسَاعِدَنَا.

The Bull shook its long tail and said, "I have four strong and fast legs."
"I am also a quick sprinter," the horse added.
The rooster looked down in sorrow and muttered, "I've got two little legs so I can't run fast, and I have wings but can't fly."
 "Although I have four legs, I'm still very slow," the lamb joined.
"We will work as a team," the horse replied. "I will carry the rooster on my back and bull will carry the little lamb." "I will search for Bear to help us," the Ostrich said.

طَارَتِ البَطَّةُ وَفِي مِنقَارِهَا بَعضُ الحِجَارَةِ تَرمِيهَا عَلَى التِّمسَاحِ.. غَضِبَ التِّمسَاحُ، وَسَبَحَ بِاتِّجَاهِهَا مُحَاوِلًا إِمسَاكَهَا، بَينَمَا تَسَلَّلَ الأَصدِقَاءُ مِن خَلفِ التِّمسَاحِ، وَبَدَؤُوا بِعُبُورِ النَّهرِ، وَفَجأَةً وَهُم فِي وَسَطِ النَّهرِ التَفَتَ التِّمسَاحُ خَلفَهُ، وَرَأَى الأَصدِقَاءَ، حَرَّكَ ذَيلَهُ الطَّوِيلَ مُسرِعًا بِاتِّجَاهِهِم، وَصَارَ الدِّيكُ يَصِيحُ بِخَوفٍ: التِّمسَاحُ قَادِمٌ بِاتِّجَاهِنَا.

Armed with stones in her beak, the duck flew in the distance. One by one, she threw the stones down at the crocodile. He was furious and followed her in an attempt to catch her.

During this time, the friends crept from behind the crocodile and crossed the river reaching midway. The crocodile suddenly turned around and saw the friends.he moved his long tail and quickly swam towards them.

The rooster was crowing with fear, "The crocodile is coming towards us!"

فَجْأَةً! تَوَقَّفَ التِّمْسَاحُ، وَصَارَ يَسْبَحُ بَعِيدًا عَنْهُم، اسْتَغْرَبَ الأَصْدِقَاءُ مِنْ ذَلِكَ، ثُمَّ الْتَفَتُوا خَلْفَهُم فَرَأَوْا الدُّبَّ يَقْفِزُ إِلَى النَّهْرِ بِاتِّجَاهِهِم.

ابْتَهَجَ الأَصْدِقَاءُ بِانْتِصَارِهِم كَثِيرًا، وَقَالَتِ النَّعَامَةُ: إِنَّ التَّعَاوُنَ عَلَى حَلِّ الْمُشْكِلَاتِ هُوَ السَّبِيلُ الأَفْضَلُ لِلنَّجَاةِ مِنَ الْمَخَاطِرِ.

Suddenly, the crocodile stopped and turned away from them. The friends were surprised and looked at each other; they turned to see Bear jumping into the river towards them.
The friends rejoiced at their victory.
"Working as a team is truly the best way to survive dangers!" the Ostrich exclaimed.

أَغْلَقَ الأَبُ الكِتَابَ، ثُمَّ سَأَلَهُم: هَل أَعْجَبَتْكُمُ القِصَّةَ؟

قَالَ يُوسُفُ: نَعَم.. أَعْجَبَتْنِي كَثِيرًا، وَأَيْضًا بِالتَّعَاوُنِ نَجْلُبُ السَّعَادَةَ، وَنُوَفِّرُ الوَقْتَ وَالجُهْدَ.

قَالَ الأَبُ: أَحْسَنتَ يَا يُوسُفُ.

قَالَت لِينَا: شُكرًا لَكَ يَا أَبِي، إِنَّهَا قِصَّةٌ جَمِيلَةٌ وَمُفِيدَةٌ.

Father closed the book. "Did you like the story?" he asked.
"Yes, I like it a lot!" Yousef replied. "Teamwork also brings happiness and saves time and energy."
"Well done, Yousef," Father praised.
"Thank you, it's a lovely and useful story," Leena said.

أَخَذَ أَحْمَدُ نَفَسًا عَمِيقًا، ثُمَّ قَامَ عَنِ الأَرِيكَةِ وَقَالَ: سَوْفَ أَبْدَأُ مِنَ اليَوْمِ بِالتَّعَاوُنِ مَعَ أُمِّي وَأَبِي وَمُسَاعَدَتِهِم.
سَمِعَتِ الأُمُّ كَلَامَهُ وَهِيَ تَدْخُلُ الغُرْفَةَ، فَقَالَت: أَحْسَنْتَ يَأَحْمَدُ.. ثُمَّ وَضَعَت أَمَامَهُم بَعْضَ المُثَلَّجَاتِ، وَالمُهَلَّبِيَّةَ.
قَالَ الأَبُ: أَنَا أُفَضِّلُ الفَوَاكِهَ، سَوْفَ أُحْضِرُ بَعْضًا مِنهَا.
قَالَتِ الأُمُّ بِمَحَبَّةٍ: شُكْرًا لَكُم جَمِيعًا عَلَى تَعَاوُنِكُم.

Ahmad inhaled deeply as he got up from the sofa. "From today, I will start working as a team – I will help my parents with chores around the house," he said eagerly. As Mother was walking into the room with some ice cream and pudding, she heard Ahmad's words and replied with a smile, "Well done, Ahmad!"
"I prefer some fruit," Father said. "I will go and bring some."
"Thank you all for working as a team!" Mother praised lovingly.

Index

English	Arabic	English	Arabic
Bull	ثَوْرٌ	Teamwork	العَمَلُ الجَمَاعِي
Horse	حِصَانٌ	Sofa	أَرِيكَةِ
Ostrich	نَعَامَةِ	Dining Table	طَاوِلَةِ الطَّعَامِ
Bear	دُبٌ	Chair	كُرْسِي
Rooster	دِيكٌ	Plate	صَحْن
Lamb	حَمَلُ	Spoon	مِلْعَقَةٌ
Duck	بَطَّةٌ	Fork	شَوكَة
Turtle	سُلْحَفَاة	Knife	سِكِين
Crocodile	تِمْسَاحٌ	Tray	صِينِيَة
Furry	فَرْو	Bottle of Water	قِنِينَةَ المَاءِ
Feathers	رِيش	Cups	الأكْوَابِ
Tail	ذَيْل	Food	الطَّعَام
Hooves	حَوَافِر	Rice	رُزٌّ
Horns	قَرْنَان	Chicken	الدَّجَاج
Beak	مُنْقَار	Aubergine	البَاذِنْجَان
Wings	جَنَاحَان	Courgette	الكُوسَا
Legs	أَرْجُلٍ	Potatoes	البَطَاطَا
Green	أَخْضَر	Fried	المَقْلِيَّة
Grey	رَمَادِي	Salad	السَّلَطَة
Brown	بُنِّي	Cucumber	الخِيَار
Red	أَحْمَر	Tomato	الطَّمَاطِم
Black	أَسْود	Lettuce	الخَسِّ
White	أَبْيَض	Green Pepper	الفُلْفُلَ الأخْضَرَ
Yellow	صَفْرَاء	Salt	المِلْحَ
Delicious	لَذِيذٌ	Lemon Juice	عَصِير اللَّيْمُون
Large	كَبِير	Bread	الخُبْز
Small	صَغِيرَةٍ	Ice-Cream	المُثَلَّجَاتِ
Beautiful	جَمِيلَة	Budding	المُهَلِّبِيَّة
Short	قَصِير	Fruits	الفَوَاكِة
Long	طَوِيلٌ	Please	مِنْ فَضْلِكَ
Slow	بَطِيئَةً	Thank you	شُكْرًا لَكُم
Fast	سَرِيعَةٌ	Time	الوَقْت
Predatory	مُفْتَرِس	Farm	المَزْرَعَةِ
Evil	شِرِيرٌ	Forest	الغَابَةُ
Strong	قَوِيَة	River	نَهْر
Delicious	لَذِيذٌ		

Top tip after reading

Encourage learners to use Arabic terms in their daily life.

Questions about the story:

Discuss the story with learners. You may ask questions like:

- What is the moral of the story?
- Why is 'Teamwork' important?
- Why were the animals scared?
- Which part of the story did you most enjoy/least enjoy?
- Are you able to use some of the Arabic terms in your own sentences?

Play a game

Point your finger at one of the English words and then ask the learner to find the meaning in Arabic, play more than one time.